The Ambiguicon:

Quips & Quotations

Stephen Hoover

and

L.A. Laird

The Ambiguicon: Quips & Quotations

6699

I hate quotations.

Ralph Waldo Emerson

The surest way to make a monkey of a man is to quote him.

Robert Benchley

She had a pretty gift for quotation, which is a serviceable substitute for wit.

W. Somerset Maughum

It is a good thing for an uneducated man to read books of quotations.

Winston Churchill

Few people can be happy unless they hate some other person, nation, or creed.

Bertrand Russell

Living with a saint is more grueling than being one.

Robert Neville

He was of the faith chiefly in the sense that the church he currently did not attend was Catholic.

Kingsley Amis

I'm astounded by people who want to know the universe when it's hard enough to know your way around Chinatown.

Woody Allen

It is better to know some of the questions than all of the answers.

James Thurber

I have a new philosophy. I am only going to dread one day at a time.

Charles Schulz

There is more to life than increasing its speed.

Mahatma Gandhi

Life is like playing a violin in public and learning the instrument as one goes on.

Samuel Butler

Life is what happens while you are making other plans.

John Lennon

After I'm dead I'd rather have people ask why I have no monument than why I have one.

Cato the Elder

For three days after death hair and fingernails continue to grow but phone calls taper off.

Johnny Carson

If once a man indulges himself in murder, very soon he comes to think little of robbing; and from robbing he next comes to drinking and Sabbath- breaking, and from that to incivility and procrastination.

Thomas De Quincey

There is no money in poetry, but then there is no poetry in money, either.

Robert Graves

This poem will never reach its destination.

Voltaire

he intelligent man finds almost everything ridiculous, the sensible man hardly anything.

Johann Wolfgang von Goethe

I'm going to speak my mind because I have nothing to lose.

S. I. Hayakawa

For every ten jokes, thou has got an hundred enemies.

Laurence Sterne

Wit is educated insolence.

Aristotle

He who laughs, lasts.

Mary Pettibone Poole

Only the mediocre are always at their best.

Jean Giraudoux

Man: An animal [whose] . . . chief occupation is extermination of other animals and his own species, which, however, multiplies with such insistent rapidity as to infest the whole habitable earth and Canada.

Ambrose Bierce

Woman: An animal . . . having a rudimentary susceptibility to domestication . . . The species is the most widely distributed of all beasts of prey. . . . The woman is omnivorous and can be taught not to talk.

Ambrose Bierce

Familiarity breeds attempt.

Goodman Ace

If it weren't for pickpockets I'd have no sex life at all.

Rodney Dangerfield

A woman occasionally is quite a serviceable substitute for masturbation.

Karl Kraus

What men desire is a virgin who is a whore.

Edward Dahlberg

To love oneself is the beginning of a life-long romance.

Oscar Wilde

The orgasm has replaced the Cross as the focus of longing and the image of fulfillment.

Malcolm Muggeridge

Love is an ocean of emotions entirely surrounded by expenses.

Lord Dewar

A man can be happy with any woman as long as he does not love her.

Oscar Wilde

Seriousness is the only refuge of the shallow.

Oscar Wilde

Egotist: A person more interested in himself than in me.

Ambrose Bierce

A narcissist is someone better looking than you are.

Gore Vidal

Don't be humble. You're not that great.

Golda Meir

To enter life by way of the vagina is as good a way as any.

Henry Miller

I have an intense desire to return to the womb. Anybody's.

Woody Allen

To my embarrassment I was born in bed with a lady.

Wilson Mizner

I knew I was an unwanted baby when I saw that my bath toys were a toaster and a radio.

Joan Rivers

All children are essentially criminal.

Denis Diderot

There was a time when we expected nothing of children but obedience, as opposed to the present, when we expect everything of them but obedience.

Anatole Broyard

The reason grandparents and grandchildren get along so well is that they have a common enemy.

Sam Levenson

I hate women because they always know where things are.

James Thurber

It takes a woman twenty years to make a man of her son, and another woman twenty minutes to make a fool of him.

Helen Rowland

It is better to have loved and lost than never to have lost at all.

Samuel Butler

If I ever marry it will be on a sudden impulse, as a man shoots himself

An archeologist is the best husband a woman can have; the older she gets, the more interested he is in her.

Agatha Christie

Don't let it end like this. Tell them I said something. Last words of

Pancho Villa

It is better to be a coward for a minute than dead for the rest of your life.

Irish proverb

The reverse side also has a reverse side.

Japanese proverb

Tell the truth and run.

Yugoslavian proverb

Do not insult the mother alligator until after you have crossed the river.

Haitian proverb

Too clever is dumb.

German proverb

When the cat and mouse agree, the grocer is ruined.

Persian proverb

Wise men make proverbs but fools repeat them.

Samuel Palmer

A bird in the hand was worth two in the bush, he told her, to which she retorted that a proverb was the last refuge of the mentally destitute.

W. Somerset Maugham

For even when we were with you, this we commanded you, that if any would not work, neither should he eat.

2 Thessalonians 3:10 (KJV).

Nobody has ever bet enough on the winning horse. Overheard at a racetrack

Richard Sasuly

You might as well fall flat on your face as lean over too far backward.

James Thurber

Alexander III of Macedonia is known as Alexander the Great because he killed more people of more different kinds than any other man of his time.

Will Cuppy

Aristotle was famous for knowing everything. He taught that the brain exists merely to cool the blood and is not involved in the process of thinking. This is true only of certain persons.

Will Cuppy

Oh, this age! How tasteless and ill-bred it is!

Catullus

How little you know about the age you live in if you think that honey is sweeter than cash in hand.

Ovid

The school of hard knocks is an accelerated curriculum.

Menander

A man with his belly full of the classics is an enemy of the human race.

Henry Miller

Patriotism is the willingness to kill and be killed for trivial reasons.

Bertrand Russell

America has been discovered before, but it has always been hushed up.

Oscar Wilde

A government which robs Peter to pay Paul can always depend on the support of Paul.

George Bernard Shaw

I know not, sir, whether Bacon wrote the works of Shakespeare, but if he did not it seems to me that he missed the opportunity of his life.

James Barrie

Henry James writes fiction as if it were a painful duty.

Oscar Wilde

Why do writers write? Because it isn't there.

Thomas Berger

Never let a domestic quarrel ruin a day's writing. If you - can't start the next day fresh, get rid of your wife.

One of Mario Puzo's rules for writing a best-selling novel.

Every novel should have a beginning, a muddle, and an end.

Peter De Vries

Boy meets girl; girl gets boy into pickle; boy gets pickle into girl.

Jack Woodford on plotting

Writing is easy. All you do is stare at a blank sheet of paper until drops of blood form on your forehead.

Gene Fowler

In literature as in love, we are astonished at what is chosen by others.

André Maurois

I used to be treated like an idiot, now I'm treated like an idiot savant.

Martin Cruz Smith after his novel Gorky Park became a best seller

Marry money.

Max Shulman's advice to aspiring authors.

Writer are just shmucks with Underwoods.

Jack Warner

The man who reads nothing at all is better educated than the man who reads nothing but newspapers.

Thomas Jefferson

Journalism largely consists in saying "Lord Jones is dead" to people who never knew Lord Jones was alive.

G. K. Chesterton

There is so much to be said in favor of modern journalism. By giving us the opinions of the uneducated it keeps us in touch with the ignorance of the community.

Oscar Wilde

Most writers regard the truth as their most valuable possession, and therefore are most economical in its use.

Mark Twain

If you can't annoy somebody, there is little point in writing.

Kingsley Amis

Unprovided with original learning, unformed in the habits of thinking, unskilled in the arts of composition, I resolved to write a book.

Edward Gibbon

Everywhere I go I'm asked if I think the university stifles writers. My opinion is that they don't stifle enough of them.

Flannery O'Connor

I write fiction because it's a way of making statements I can disown, and I write plays because dialogue is the most respectable way of contradicting myself.

Tom Stoppard

An author's first duty is to let down his country.

Brendan Behan

Asking a working writer what he thinks about critics is like asking a lamp-post how it feels about dogs.

Christopher Hampton

A poem is never finished, only abandoned.

Paul Valéry

Immature poets imitate; mature poets steal.

T. S. Eliot

Good swiping is an art in itself.

Jules Feifferr

Finishing a book is just like you took a child out in the back yard and shot it.

Truman Capote

You call this a script? Give me a couple of 5,000-dollar-a-week writers and I'll write it myself.

Movie producer Joe Pasternak

I do most of my writing sitting down. That's where I shine.

Robert Benchley

When in doubt, have two guys come through the door with guns.

Raymond Chandler

T'was a woman who drove me to drink, and I never had the courtesy to thank her for it.

W. C. Fields

My uncle was the town drunk—and we lived in Chicago.

George Gobel

I drink to make other people more interesting.

George Jean Nathan

People always talk about my drinking but never my thirst.

Scottish proverb

Water, taken in moderation, cannot hurt anybody.

Mark Twain

If you drink, don't drive. Don't even putt.

Dean Martin

One more drink and I'll be under the host.

> *Dorothy Parker*

Sometimes too much to drink is barely enough.

> *Mark Twain*

I tremble for my country when I reflect that God is just.

> *Thomas Jefferson*

If you weren't such a great man you'd be a terrible bore.

> *Mrs. William Gladstone to her husband.*

He speaks to me as if I were a public meeting.

> *Queen Victoria on Gladstone.*

I never trust a man unless I've got his pecker in my pocket.

> *Lyndon Johnson*

Ronald Reagan is not a typical politician because he doesn't know how to lie, cheat, and steal. He's always had an agent for that.

> *Bob Hope*

When I was a boy I was told that anybody could become President; I'm beginning to believe it.

Clarence Darrow

I'd rather entrust the government of the United States to the first 400 people listed in the Boston telephone directory than to the faculty of Harvard University.

William F. Buckley, Jr.

The only thing that saves us from the bureaucracy is its inefficiency.

Eugene McCarthy

Henry James chews more than he bites off.

Mrs. Henry Adams

The mistakes are all there, waiting to be made.

Chess master Savielly Tartakower

I don't jog. If I die I want to be sick.

Abe Lemons

Be careful about reading health books. You may die of a misprint.

Mark Twain

It is unbecoming for young men to utter maxims.

Aristotle

Never go to a doctor whose office plants have died.

Erma Bombeck

I suppose one has a greater sense of intellectual degradation after an interview with a doctor than from any human experience.

Alice James

A young doctor means a new graveyard.

German proverb

I'm going to Boston to see my doctor. He's a very sick man.

Fred Allen

Before undergoing a surgical operation, arrange your temporal affairs. You may live.

Ambrose Bierce

Psychoanalysis is that mental illness for which it regards itself a therapy.

Karl Kraus

The doctor can bury his mistakes but an architect can only advise his client to plant vines.

Frank Lloyd Wright

I'm lonesome. They are all dying. I have hardly a warm personal enemy left.

James McNeill Whistler

Nothing is said that has not been said before.

Terence

Only the shallow know themselves.

Oscar Wilde

It's no longer a question of staying healthy. It's a question of finding a sickness you like.

Jackie Mason

As for me, except for an occasional heart attack, I feel as young as I ever did.

Robert Benchley

I get my exercise acting as a pallbearer to my friends who exercise.

Chauncey Depew

Quit worrying about your health. It'll go away.

Robert Orben

We all have the strength to endure the misfortunes of others.

La Rochefoucauld

I've always been interested in people, but I've never liked them.

Somerset Maugham

One of the symptoms of an approaching nervous breakdown is the belief that one's work is terribly important.

Bertrand Russell

A little inaccuracy sometimes saves tons of explanation.

H. H. Munro (Saki)

Three o'clock is always too late or too early for anything you want to do.

Jean-Paul Sartre

Virtue is its own revenge.

E. Y. Harburg

A good deed never goes unpunished.

Gore Vidal

M an is the only animal that laughs and has a state legislature.

Samuel Butler

More than any time in history mankind faces a crossroads. One path leads to despair and utter hopelessness, the other to total extinction. Let us pray that we have the wisdom to choose correctly.

Woody Allen

It is dangerous to be sincere unless you are also stupid.

George Bernard Shaw

If you haven't got anything nice to say about anybody, come sit next to me.

Alice Roosevelt Longworth

I'm as pure as the driven slush.

Tallulah Bankhead

The race may not be to the swift nor the victory to the strong, but that's the way to bet.

Damon Runyon

I don't trust him. We're friends.

Bertolt Brecht

A man can't be too careful in the choice of his enemies.

Oscar Wilde

It was such a lovely day I thought it was a pity to get up.

Somerset Maugham

I go to the theater to be entertained. I don't want to see rape, sodomy, and drug addiction. I can get all that at home.

Alan Bennett

I may have my faults, but being wrong ain't one of them.

Jimmy Hoffa

Forgive your enemies, but never forget their names.

John F. Kennedy

There is no pleasure in having nothing to do; the fun is having lots to do and not doing it.

John W. Raper

Hope is the feeling you have that the feeling you have isn't permanent.

Jean Kerr

Success didn't spoil me; I've always been insufferable.

Fran Lebowitz

If this is coffee, please bring me some tea; but if this is tea, please bring me some coffee.

Abraham Lincoln

Reality is a crutch for people who can't cope with drugs.

Lily Tomlin

Anyone who eats three meals a day should understand why cookbooks outsell sex books three to one.

L. M. Boyd

If my film makes one more person miserable, I'll feel I've done my job.

Woody Allen

So little time and so little to do.

Oscar Levant

A kleptomaniac is a person who helps himself because he can't help himself.

Oscar Levant

From birth to age 18, a girl needs good parents; from 18 to 35 she needs good looks; from 35 to 55 she needs a good personality; from 55 on she needs cash.

Sophie Tucker

When I hear the word "culture" I reach for my gun.

Hans Johst

A question that sometimes drives me hazy: Am I or the others crazy?

Albert Einstein

The only normal people are the ones you don't know very well.

Joe Ancis

I like men to behave like men — strong and childish.

Françoise Sagan Henry Morgan

A hypocrite is a person who—but who isn't?

Don Marquis

Everything has been figured out except how to live.

Jean-Paul Sartre

Howard Hughes was able to afford the luxury of madness, like a man who not only thinks he is Napoleon but hires an army to prove it.

Ted Morgan

When it is not necessary to make a decision, it is necessary not to make a decision.

Lord Falkland

T his book fills a much-needed gap.

Moses Hadas

Thank you for sending me a copy of your book. I'll waste no time reading it.

Moses Hadas

There's no thief like a bad book.

Italian proverb

The man who doesn't read good books has no advantage over the man who can't read them.

Mark Twain

Studying literature at Harvard is like learning about women at the Mayo Clinic.

Roy Blount, Jr.

One, two, three, Buckle my shoe.

Robert Benchley

I've given up reading books. I find it takes my mind off myself.

Oscar Levant

Where do I find the time for not reading so many books?

Karl Kraus

The reason why so few good books are written is that so few people who can write know anything.

Walter Bagehot

Manuscript: Something submitted in haste and returned at leisure.

Oliver Herford

Your manuscript is both good and original, but the part that is good is not original and the part that is original is not good.

Samuel Johnson

A well-written life is almost as rare as a well- spent one.

Thomas Carlyle

I have read your book and much like it.

Moses Hadas

There are two kinds of books: those that no one reads and those that no one ought to read.

H. L. Mencken

The covers of this book are too far apart.

Ambrose Bierce

There are plenty of good five-cent cigars in the country. The trouble is they cost a quarter. What this country really needs is a good five-cent nickel.

Franklin P. Adams

Being perfectly well-dressed gives a feeling of tranquility that religion is powerless to bestow.

Ralph Waldo Emerson

We are here and it is now. Further than that all human knowledge is moonshine .

H. L. Mencken

Don't get the idea that I'm knocking the American system.

Al Capone

Truth is beautiful, without doubt; but so are lies.

Ralph Waldo Emerson

There are more of them than us.

Herb Caen

Never go to bed mad. Stay up and fight.

Phyllis Diller

I never lecture, not because I am shy or a bad speaker, but simply because I detest the sort of people who go to lectures and don't want to meet them.

H. L. Mencken

I improve on misquotation.

Cary Grant

Honest criticism is hard to take, particularly from a relative, a friend, an acquaintance, or a stranger.

Franklin P. Jones

It is more important to have steady income than to be interesting.

Oscar Wilde

France was a long despotism tempered by epigrams.

Thomas Carlyle

Victory goes to the player who makes the next-to- last mistake.

Chess master Savielly Tartakower

It is rather to be chosen than great riches, unless I have omitted something from the quotation.

Robert Benchley

There must be 500,000 rats in the United States; of course, I am only speaking from memory.

Bill Nye

Lord Ronald said nothing; he flung himself from the room, flung himself upon his horse and rode madly off in all directions.

Stephen Leacock

We can't all be heroes because somebody has to sit on the curb and clap as they go by.

Will Rogers

Some things have to be believed to be seen.

Ralph Hodgson on ESP

Middle age is when you've met so many people that every new person you meet reminds you of someone else.

Ogden Nash

Wagner's music is better than it sounds.

Bill Nye

I don't want any yes-men around me. I want everybody to tell me the truth even if it costs them their jobs.

Samuel Goldwyn

The advantage of the emotions is that they lead us astray.

Oscar Wilde

Underneath this flabby exterior is an enormous lack of character.

Oscar Levant

Nobody roots for Goliath.

Wilt Chamberlain

Tradition is what you resort to when you don't have the time or the money to do it right.

Kurt Herbert Adler

All truths are half-truths. Alfred

North Whitehead

Why attack God? He may be as miserable as we are.

Erik Satie

Christ died for our sins. Dare we make his martyrdom meaningless by not committing them?

Jules Feiffer

The last time I saw him he was walking down Lover's Lane holding his own hand.

Fred Allen

The nice thing about egotists is that they don't talk about other people.

Lucille S. Harper

If I love you, what business is it of yours?

Johann Wolfgang von Goethe

I used to be Snow White, but I drifted.

Mae West

He who hesitates is a damned fool.

Mae West

Contraceptives should be used on every conceivable occasion.

Spike Milligan

It's been so long since I made love I can't even remember who gets tied up.

Joan Rivers

A man can sleep around, no questions asked, but if a woman makes nineteen or twenty mistakes she's a tramp.

Joan Rivers

Monogamy is the Western custom of one wife and hardly any mistresses.

H. H. Munro (Saki)

A man in love is incomplete until he is married. Then he is finished.

Zsa Zsa Gabor

When a girl marries she exchanges the attentions of many men for the inattention of one.

Helen Rowland

The most happy marriage I can imagine to myself would be the union of a deaf man to a blind woman.

Samuel Taylor Coleridge

Marriage has driven more than one man to sex.

Peter De Vries

Dating means doing a lot of fun things you will never do again if you get married. The fun stops with marriage because you're trying to save money for when you split up your property.

Dave Barry

Marriage is like paying an endless visit in your worst clothes.

J. B. Priestley

Marriage is like a besieged fortress. Everyone outside wants to get in, and everyone inside wants to get out.

P. M. Quitard

The chains of marriage are so heavy it takes two to carry them, and sometimes three.

Alexandre Dumas

Instead of getting married again, I'm going to find a woman I don't like and give her a house.

Lewis Grizzard

My divorce came as a complete surprise to me. That will happen when you haven't been home in eighteen years.

Lee Trevino

Conrad Hilton was very generous to me in the divorce settlement. He gave me 5,000 Gideon Bibles.

Zsa Zsa Gabor

Always get married early in the morning. That way, if it doesn't work out, you haven't wasted a whole day.

Mickey Rooney

My wife and I were happy for twenty years. Then we met.

Rodney Dangerfield

I grew up in a very large family in a very small house. I never slept alone until after I was married.

Lewis Grizzard

Monogamous and monotonous are synonymous.

Thaddeus Golas

A wife lasts only for the length of the marriage, but an ex-wife is there for the rest of your life.

Jim Samuels

Bachelors should be heavily taxed. It is not fair that some men should be happier than others.

Oscar Wilde

Marriage is based on the theory that when a man discovers a brand of beer exactly to his taste he should at once throw up his job and go to work in the brewery.

George Jean Nathan

It destroys one's nerves to be amiable every day to the same human being.

Benjamin Disraeli

Marriage is like a bank account. You put it in, you take it out, you lose interest.

Professor Irwin Corey

The trouble with incest is that it gets you involved with relatives.

George S. Kaufman

I was thrown out of college for cheating on the metaphysics exam; I looked into the soul of the boy next to me.

Woody Allen

The most popular labor-saving device today is still a husband with money.

Joey Adams

Defeat is worse than death because you have to live with defeat.

Bill Musselman

Whatever women do they must do twice as well as men to be thought half as good. Luckily, this is not difficult.

Charlotte Whitton

I believe in sex and death—two experiences that come once in a lifetime.

Woody Allen

A gentleman never strikes a lady with his hat on.

Fred Allen

I've never struck a woman in my life, not even my own mother.

W. C. Fields

I'm not a real movie star — I've still got the same wife I started out with twenty-eight years ago.

Will Rogers

I am a deeply superficial person.

Andy Warhol

Nothing succeeds like the appearance of success.

Christopher Lasch

She's the kind of girl who climbed the ladder of success wrong by wrong.

Mae West

Nothing fails like success.

Gerald Nachman

You may already be a loser.

Form letter received by Rodney Dangerfield

How should they answer?

Abigail Van Buren
...in reply to the question "Why do Jews always answer a question with a question? "

I want to be the white man's brother, not his brother-in-law.

Martin Luther King, Jr.

I have just enough white in me to make my honesty questionable.

Will Rogers

I never believed in Santa Claus because I knew no white dude would come into my neighborhood after dark.

Dick Gregory

Work is of two kinds: first, altering the position of matter at or near the earth's surface relative to other matter; second, telling other people to do so.

Bertrand Russell

It is impossible to enjoy idling unless there is plenty of work to do.

Jerome K. Jerome

Hard work never killed anybody -- but why take a chance?

Charlie McCarthy

The trouble with the rat race is that even if you win you're still a rat.

Lily Tomlin

A billion here, a billion there — pretty soon it adds up to real money.

Senator Everett Dirksen

I have enough money to last me the rest of my life, unless I buy something.

Jackie Mason

Money is always there, but the pockets change.

Gertrude Stein

There must be more to life than having everything.

Maurice Sendak

Save a little money each month and at the end of the year -- you'll be surprised at how little you have.

Ernest Haskins

My problem lies in reconciling my gross habits with my net income.

Errol Flynn

Any man who has $10,000 left when he dies is a failure.

Errol Flynn

I

'm living so far beyond my income that we may almost be said to be living apart.

e. e. cummings

F ashion is a form of ugliness so intolerable that we have to alter it every six months.

Oscar Wilde

Every generation laughs at the old fashions but religiously follows the new.

Henry David Thoreau

War is a series of catastrophes that results in a victory.

Georges Clemenceau

You can no more win a war than you can win an earthquake.

Jeannette Rankin

The object of war is not to die for your country but to make the other bastard die for his.

General George Patton

Name me an emperor who was ever struck by a cannon-ball.

Charles V

You can't say civilization don't advance, because in every war they kill you a new way.

Will Rogers

I have already given two cousins to the war and I stand ready to sacrifice my wife's brother.

Artemus Ward

Start slow and taper off.

Walt Stack

I don't deserve this award, but I have arthritis and I don't deserve that either.

Jack Benny

The best way to keep one's word is not to give it.

Napoleon

It's all right letting yourself go as long as you can let yourself back.

Mick Jagger

T o eat is human. To digest divine.

Mark Twain

I don't even butter my bread. I consider that cooking.

Katherine Cebrian

There is no sincerer love than the love of food.

George Bernard Shaw

The most dangerous food is wedding cake.

American proverb

The two biggest sellers in any bookstore are the cookbooks and the diet books. The cookbooks tell you how to prepare the food and the diet books tell you how not to eat any of it.

Andy Rooney

I eat merely to put food out of my mind.

N. F. Simpson

Poets have been mysteriously silent on the subject of cheese.

G. K. Chesterton

The most remarkable thing about my mother is that for thirty years she served the family nothing but leftovers. The original meal has never been found.

Calvin Trillin

No man is lonely while eating spaghetti.

Robert Morley

The trouble with life in the fast lane is that you get to the other end in an awful hurry.

John Jensen

It is not true that life is one damn thing after another — it is one damn thing over and over.

Edna St. Vincent Millay

Life is thirst.

Leonard Michaels

The less things change, the more they stay the same.

Sicilian proverb

There are days when it takes all you've got just to keep up with the losers.

Robert Orben

If you can see the light at the end of the tunnel you are looking the wrong way.

Barry Commoner

I have found little that is good about human beings. In my experience most of them are trash.

Sigmund Freud

The brotherhood of man is not a mere poet's dream; it is a most depressing and humiliating reality.

Oscar Wilde

We're all in this alone.

Lily Tomlin

Our ignorance of history makes us libel our own times. People have always been like this.

Gustave Flaubert

France is a country where the money falls apart and you can't tear the toilet paper.

Billy Wilder

Historians have now definitely established that Juan Cabrillo, discoverer of California, was not looking for Kansas, thus setting a precedent that continues to this day.

Wayne Shannon

New York now leads the world's great cities in the number of people around whom you shouldn't make a sudden move.

David Letterman

It isn't necessary to have relatives in Kansas City in order to be unhappy.

Groucho Marx

Isn't it nice that people who prefer Los Angeles to San Francisco live there?

Herb Caen

When we talk to God, we're praying. When God talks to us, we're schizophrenic.

Lily Tomlin

When dealing with the insane, the best method is to pretend to be sane.

Hermann Hesse

Opera in English is, in the main, just about as sensible as baseball in Italian.

H. L. Mencken

I tried to resist his overtures, but he plied me with symphonies, quartettes, chamber music, and cantatas.

S. J. Perelman

In opera anything that is too stupid to be spoken is sung.

Voltaire

No statue has ever been put up to a critic.

Jean Sibelius

Massenet

Never wrote a Mass in A.

It'd have been just too bad

If he had.

Anthony Butts

Music played at weddings always reminds me of the music played for soldiers before they go into battle.

Heinrich Heine

I don't know anything about music. In my line, you don't have to.

Elvis Presley

Hell is full of musical amateurs.

George Bernard Shaw

Rock and roll is the hamburger that ate the world.

Peter York

You can make a killing as a playwright in America, but you can't make a living.

Sherwood Anderson

I don't want to see the uncut version of anything.

Jean Kerr

Hell is a half-filled auditorium.

Robert Frost

A critic is a man who knows the way but can't drive the car.

Kenneth Tynan

Hollywood is a place where they place you under contract instead of under observation.

Walter Winchell

The Hollywood tradition I like best is called "sucking up to the stars".

Johnny Carson

"Hello," he lied.

Don Carpenter quoting a Hollywood agent

An associate producer is the only guy in Hollywood who will associate with a producer.

Fred Allen

Television has proved that people will look at anything rather than each other.

Ann Landers

Television is more interesting than people. If it were not, we would have people standing in the corners of our rooms.

Alan Coren

Television is a medium, so called because it is neither rare nor well done.

Fred Allen

Americans are a race of convicts and ought to be thankful for anything we allow them short of hanging.

Samuel Johnson

America is a large friendly dog in a small room. Every time it wags its tail it knocks over a chair.

Arnold Toynbee

In America there are two classes of travel—first and with children.

Robert Benchley

Reagan won because he ran against Jimmy Carter. Had he run unopposed he would have lost.

Mort Sahl

The vice-presidency ain't worth a bucket of warm piss.

Vice President John Nance Garner

Every decent man is ashamed of the government he lives under.

H. L. Mencken

A statesman is a politician who has been dead ten or fifteen years.

Harry S Truman

When you go into court you are putting your fate into the hands of twelve people who weren't smart enough to get out of jury duty.

Norm Crosby

Laws are like sausages. It's better not to see them being made.

Otto von Bismarck

I always turn to the sports pages first, which record - people's accomplishments. The front page has nothing but man's failures.

Chief Justice Earl Warren

I f we see the light at the end of the tunnel, it's the light of an oncoming train.

Robert Lowell

Ninety percent of *everything* is crap.

Science fiction writer Theodore Sturgeon
(after being told "Ninety percent of science fiction is crap")

Man is the only animal that can remain on friendly terms with the victims he intends to eat until he eats them.

Samuel Butler

Cats are intended to teach us that not everything in nature has a function.

Garrison Keillor

You've always made the mistake of being yourself.

Eugène Ionesco

All phone calls are obscene.

Karen Elizabeth Gordon

Coincidences are spiritual puns.

G. K. Chesterton

I have a hundred times wished that one could resign life as an officer resigns a commission.

Robert Burns

If you tell the truth you don't have to remember anything.

Mark Twain

The more he talked of his honor the faster we counted our spoons.

Ralph Waldo Emerson

No one can have a higher opinion of him than I have, and I think he's a dirty little beast.

W. S. Gilbert

The future is much like the present, only longer.

Dan Quisenberry

Weather forecast for tonight: dark.

George Carlin

A person can take only so much comforting.

Calvin Trillin

Illegal aliens have always been a problem in the United States. Ask any Indian.

Robert Orben

Few things are harder to put up with than a good example.

Mark Twain

Hell is other people.

Jean-Paul Sartre

The popularity of a bad man is as treacherous as he is himself.

Pliny the Younger (c. 62–c. 113)

The hatred of relatives is the most violent.

Tacitus (c. 55–c. 117)

Every man sees in his relatives a series of grotesque caricatures of himself.

H. L. Mencken

H. L. Mencken suffers from the hallucination that he is H. L. Mencken. There is no cure for a disease of that magnitude.

Maxwell Bodenheim

Even if you're on the right track, you'll get run over if you just sit there.

Will Rogers

Let others praise ancient times; I am glad I was born in these.

Ovid (43 B.C.–A.D. 18)

Happiness is good health and a bad memory.

Ingrid Bergman

Never keep up with the Joneses. Drag them down to your level.

Quentin Crisp

A lie is an abomination unto the Lord and a very present help in time of trouble.

Adlai Stevenson

❧

During carnival men put masks over their masks.

Xavier Forneret

One hundred thousand lemmings can't be wrong.

Graffiti

There is something about a closet that makes a skeleton terribly restless.

Wilson Mizner

Modern art is what happens when painters stop looking at girls and persuade themselves that they have a better idea.

John Ciardi

Either this wallpaper goes or I do.

The last words of Ronald Firbank

A life spent making mistakes is not only more honorable but more useful than a life spent doing nothing.

George Bernard Shaw

Friends may come and go, but enemies accumulate.

Thomas Jones

Start every day off with a smile and get it over with.

W. C. Fields

I used to work in a fire hydrant factory. You couldn't park anywhere near the place.

Steven Wright

When smashing monuments, save the pedestals— they always come in handy.

Stanislaw Lem

Great men are not always idiots.

Karen Elizabeth Gordon

Few great men could pass Personnel.

Paul Goodman

Fanaticism consists of redoubling your effort when you have forgotten your aim.

George Santayana

Nothing is more conducive to peace of mind than not having any opinions at all.

Georg Christoph Lichtenberg

It is easier to forgive an enemy than to forgive a friend.

William Blake

You are no bigger than the things that annoy you.

Jerry Bundsen

It is unpleasant to go alone, even to be drowned.

Russian proverb

We are what we pretend to be.

Kurt Vonnegut, Jr.

A language is a dialect with an army and navy.

Max Weinreich

There is only one word for aid that is genuinely without strings, and that word is blackmail.

Colm Brogan

Very few people do anything creative after the age of thirty-five. The reason is that very few people do anything creative before the age of thirty-five.

Joel Hildebrand

I think it would be a good idea.

Mahatma Gandhi,
...when asked what he thought of Western civilization

Computers are useless. They can only give you answers.

Pablo Picasso

Peace, n. In international affairs, a period of cheating between two periods of fighting.

Ambrose Bierce

The art of not reading is extremely important. It consists in our not taking up whatever happens to occupy the larger public.

Arthur Schopenhauer

Nowadays the illiterates can read and write.

Alberto Moravia

A good man is always a beginner.

Martial

The gods too are fond of a joke.

Aristotle

The only thing that stops God from sending another flood is that the first one was useless.

Nicolas Chamfort

The world is proof that God is a committee.

Bob Stokes

Which is it, is man one of God's blunders or is God one of man's?

Friedrich Nietzsche

A pious man is one who would be an atheist if the king were.

Jean de La Bruyère

I detest converts almost as much as I do missionaries.

H. L. Mencken

Life is divided into the horrible and the miserable.

Woody Allen

Of all the wild beasts of land or sea, the wildest is woman.

Menander (342?–291? B.C.)

A woman is always buying something.

Ovid (43 B.C.–A.D. 18)

Nothing is more intolerable than a wealthy woman.

Juvenal (60?–140?)

A woman talks to one man, looks at a second, and thinks of a third.

Bhartrihari, c. 625

Woman was God's second mistake.

Friedrich Nietzsche

Women are like elephants to me. I like to look at them but I wouldn't want to own one.

W. C. Fields

In love there are two evils: war and peace.

Horace (65–8 B.C.)

Love is the crocodile on the river of desire.

Bhartrihari (c. 625)

Love is what happens to men and women who don't know each other.

W. Somerset Maugham

A man always remembers his first love with special tenderness, but after that he begins to bunch them.

H. L. Mencken

Outside every thin woman is a fat man trying to get in.

Katherine Whitehorn

It is more fun contemplating somebody else's navel than your own.

Arthur Hoppe

Of all the sexual aberrations, perhaps the most peculiar is chastity.

Remy de Gourmont

Celibacy is not hereditary.

Guy Goden

Whenever I'm caught between two evils, I take the one I've never tried.

Mae West

Brains are an asset, if you hide them.

Mae West

There is so little difference between husbands you might as well keep the first.

Adela Rogers St. Johns

I am a marvelous housekeeper. Every time I leave a man I keep his house.

Zsa Zsa Gabor

The happiest time in any man's life is just after the first divorce.

John Kenneth Galbraith

I've married a few people I shouldn't have, but haven't we all?

Mamie Van Doren

What I like about masturbation is that you don't have to talk afterwards.

Milos Forman

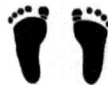

If God wanted sex to be fun, He wouldn't have included children as punishment.

Ed Bluestone

I am determined my children shall be brought up in their father 's religion, if they can find out what it is.

Charles Lamb

My mother had a great deal of trouble with me, but I think she enjoyed it.

Mark Twain

I take my children everywhere, but they always find their way back home.

Robert Orben

Never lend your car to anyone to whom you have given birth.

Erma Bombeck

Children today are tyrants. They contradict their parents, gobble their food, and tyrannize their teachers.

Socrates (470–399 B.C.)

When you are eight years old, nothing is any of your business.

Lenny Bruce

What is youth except a man or woman before it is fit to be seen?

Evelyn Waugh

I take my pet lion to church every Sunday. He has to eat.

Marty Pollio

X

Distrust any enterprise that requires new clothes.

Henry David Thoreau

I like work; it fascinates me. I can sit and look at it for hours.

Jerome K. Jerome

It is time I stepped aside for a less experienced and less able man.

Professor Scott Elledge
... upon retiring from Cornell University

The only way to succeed is to make people hate you.

Josef von Sternberg

A man can't get rich if he takes proper care of his family.

Navajo saying

The bad thing about being rich that you have to live with rich people.

Logan Pearsall Smith

Never invest in anything that eats or needs repairing.

Billy Rose

I enjoy being a highly overpaid actor.

Roger Moore

Buy old masters. They bring better prices than young mistresses.

Lord Beaverbrook

It is no disgrace to be poor, but it might as well be.

Jim Grue

An economist's guess is liable to be as good as anybody else's.

Will Rogers

Mathematics has given economics rigor, but alas, also mortis.

Robert Heilbroner

At age fifty, every man has the face he deserves.

George Orwell

The secret of staying young is to live honestly, eat slowly, and lie about your age.

Lucille Ball

I am in the prime of senility.

Joel Chandler Harris, at age 58

I am not young enough to know everything.

Oscar Wilde (1854–1900)

The closing years of life are like the end of a masquerade party, when the masks are dropped.

Arthur Schopenhauer

Old age is like a plane flying through a storm. Once you are aboard there is nothing you can do.

Golda Meir

When I was young there was no respect for the young, and now that I am old there is no respect for the old. I missed out coming and going.

J. B. Priestley

Middle age begins with the first mortgage and ends when you drop dead.

Herb Caen

$$\Rightarrow\!\!\ggg\!\!\lll\!\!\Leftarrow$$

They say such nice things about people at their funerals that it makes me sad to realize that I'm going to miss mine by just a few days.

Andy Rooney

The only thing wrong with immortality is that it tends to go on forever.

Herb Caen

The cynics are right nine times out of ten.

H. L. Mencken

What Einstein was to physics, what Babe Ruth was to home runs, what Emily Post was to table manners -- that's what Edward G. Robinson was to dying like a dirty rat.

Russell Baker

Idealism is what precedes experience; cynicism is what follows.

David T. Wolf

No matter how cynical you get, it is impossible to keep up.

Lily Tomlin

When there are two conflicting versions of a story, the wise course is to believe the one in which people appear at their worst.

H. Allen Smith

Nothing matters very much, and few things matter all.

Arthur Balfour

There is no happiness; there are only moments of happiness.

Spanish proverb

Happiness is having a large, loving, caring, close- knit family in another city.

George Burns

O Lord, help me to be pure, but not yet.

St. Augustine

A thing worth having is a thing worth cheating for.

W. C. Fields

He without benefit of scruples

His fun and money soon quadruples.

Ogden Nash

Living with a conscience is like driving a car with the brakes on.

Budd Schulberg

It has been my experience that folks who have no vices have very few virtues.

Abraham Lincoln

The price of purity is purists.

Calvin Trillin

Part of the secret of success in life is to eat what you like and let the food fight it out inside.

Mark Twain

We didn't starve, but we didn't eat chicken unless we were sick, or the chicken was.

Bernard Malamud

If you want to look young and thin, hang around old fat people.

Jim Eason

Statistics show that of those who contract the habit of eating, very few survive.

Wallace Irwin

The trouble with heart disease is that the first symptom is often hard to deal with: sudden death.

Michael Phelps, M.D.

Never give a party if you will be the most interesting person there.

Mickey Friedman

Nothing spoils a good party like a genius.

Elsa Maxwell

I will not eat oysters. I want my food dead. Not sick, not wounded. Dead.

Woody Allen

Music is essentially useless, as life is.

George Santayana

My wife and I tried to breakfast together, but we had to stop or our marriage would have been wrecked.

Winston Churchill

There is no law against composing music when one has no ideas whatsoever. The music of Wagner, therefore, is perfectly legal.

The National (Paris), 1850

Classical music is music written by famous dead foreigners.

Arlene Heath

The main thing the public demands of a composer is that he be dead.

Arthur Honegger

Do it big or stay in bed.

Opera producer Larry Kelly

A team should be an extension of the coach's personality. My teams were arrogant and obnoxious.

Al McGuire

The highlight of my baseball career came in Philadelphia's Connie Mack Stadium when I saw a fan fall out of the upper deck. When he got up and walked away the crowd booed.

Bob Uecker

I hate all sports as rabidly as a person who likes sports hates common sense.

H. L. Mencken

Art, like morality, consists of drawing the line somewhere.

G. K. Chesterton

I'm glad the old masters are all dead, and I only wish they had died sooner.

Mark Twain

Agree, for the law is costly.

William Camden

It is better to be a mouse in a cat's mouth than a man in a lawyer's hands.

Spanish proverb

Two farmers each claimed to own a certain cow. While one pulled on its head and the other pulled on its tail, the cow was milked by a lawyer.

Jewish parable

Injustice is relatively easy to bear; what stings is justice.

H. L. Mencken

I'm not an ambulance chaser. I'm usually there before the ambulance.

Melvin Belli

I never travel without my diary. One should always have something sensational to read.

Oscar Wilde

The Irish are a fair people — they never speak well of one another.

Samuel Johnson

There are still parts of Wales where the only concession to gaiety is a striped shroud.

Gwyn Thomas

California is a great place to live if you're an orange.

Fred Allen

I have just returned from Boston. It is the only thing to do if you find yourself there.

Fred Allen

Thanks to the Interstate Highway System, it is now possible to travel from coast to coast without seeing anything.

Charles Kuralt

Technology is a way of organizing the universe so that man doesn't have to experience it.

Max Frisch

Men have become the tools of their tools.

Henry David Thoreau

I thoroughly disapprove of duels. If a man should challenge me, I would take him kindly and forgivingly by the hand and lead him to a quiet place and kill him.

Mark Twain

There is nothing more exhilarating than to be shot at without result.

Winston Churchill

Nobody ever forgets where he buried the hatchet.

Kin Hubbard

You have to have a talent for having talent.

Ruth Gordon

Television is democracy at its ugliest.

Paddy Chayevsky

Television enables you to be entertained in your home by people you wouldn't have in your home.

David Frost

Imitation is the sincerest form of television.

Fred Allen

Men and nations behave wisely once they have exhausted all the other alternatives.

Abba Eban

What luck for rulers that men do not think.

Adolf Hitler

Every government is run by liars and nothing they say should be believed.

I. F. Stone

It is dangerous to be right when the government is wrong.

Voltaire

Don't burn the flag; wash it.

Norman Thomas

An honest politician is one who when he is bought will stay bought.

Simon Cameron

A communist is a person who publicly airs his dirty Lenin.

Jack Pomeroy

A conservative is a man who wants the rules changed so that no one can make a pile the way he did.

Gregory Nunn

A conservative doesn't want anything to happen for the first time; a liberal feels it should happen, but not now.

Mort Sahl

Those who are too smart to engage in politics are punished by being governed by those who are dumber.

Plato

In America, anyone can become president. That's one of the risks you take.

Adlai Stevenson

I think the American public wants a solemn ass as president. And I think I'll go along with them.

Calvin Coolidge

The only reason for being a professional writer is that you can't help it.

Leo Rosten

In Hollywood, writers are considered only the first drafts of human beings.

Frank Deford

What an author likes to write most is his signature on the back of a check.

Brendan Francis

Very few things happen at the right time and the rest do not happen at all. The conscientious historian will correct these defects.

Herodotus

History will be kind to me for I intend to write it.

Winston Churchill

It is a mean thief or a successful author that plunders the dead.

Austin O'Malley

Fiction is obliged to stick to possibilities. Truth isn't.

Mark Twain

Truth is shorter than fiction.

Irving Cohen

Get your facts first, then you can distort them as you please.

Mark Twain

Why don't you write books people can read?

Nora Joyce to her husband, James

I feel very old sometimes... I carry on and would not like to die before having emptied a few more buckets of shit on the heads of my fellow men.

Gustave Flaubert

The difference between literature and journalism is that journalism is unreadable and literature is not read.

Oscar Wilde

Advertisements contain the only truths to be relied on in a newspaper.

Thomas Jefferson

Some editors are failed writers, but so are most writers.

T. S. Eliot

Every great man has his disciples, and it is always Judas who writes the biography.

Oscar Wilde

Biography lends to death a new terror.

Oscar Wilde

It is better quotable than to be honest.

Tom Stoppard

There will be a rain dance Friday night, weather permitting.

George Carlin

Everything changes, but the avant garde.

Paul Valéry

Never mistake motion for action.

Ernest Hemingway

I wish everybody would go back into the closet.

Josef Heifetz

I'll not listen to reason. Reason always means what someone else has to say.

Elizabeth Cleghorn Gaskell

Nothing is impossible for the man who doesn't have to do it himself.

A. H. Weiler

A censor is a man who knows more than he thinks you ought to.

Granville Hicks

A s scarce as truth is, the supply has always been in excess of the demand.

Josh Billings

Anybody who thinks of going to bed before 12 o'clock is a scoundrel.

Samuel Johnson

I do not want people to be agreeable, as it saves me the trouble of liking them.

Jane Austen

A lot of people like snow. I find it to be an unnecessary freezing of water.

Carl Reiner

Often it does seem a pity that Noah and his party did not miss the boat.

Mark Twain

American college students are like American colleges — each has half-dulled faculties.

James Thurber

It took me twenty years of studied self-restraint, aided by the natural decay of my faculties, to make myself dull enough to be accepted as a serious person by the British public.

George Bernard Shaw

The longer I live the more I see that I am never wrong about anything, and that all the pains I have so humbly taken to verify my notions have only wasted my time.

George Bernard Shaw

Love thy enemies in case thy friends turn out to be a bunch of bastards. R.

A. Dickson

One should forgive one's enemies, but not before they are hanged.

Heinrich Heine

What ought to be done to the man who invented the celebrating of anniversaries? Mere killing would be too light.

Mark Twain

Never put off until tomorrow what you can do the day after tomorrow.

Mark Twain

Nobody can make you feel inferior without your consent.

Eleanor Roosevelt

Propaganda is the art of persuading others of what you don't believe yourself.

Abba Eban

Never believe anything until it has been officially denied.

Claud Cockburn

There are only two ways of telling the complete truth — anonymously and posthumously.

Thomas Sowell

ॐ

There is only one thing about which I am certain, and that is that there is very little about which one can be certain.

W. Somerset Maugham

Just because your voice reaches halfway around the world doesn't mean you are wiser than when it reached only to the end of the bar.

Edward R. Murrow

Glory is fleeting, but obscurity is forever.

Napoleon Bonaparte

It is fun being in the same decade with you.

Franklin Delano Roosevelt
…in a letter to Churchill, 1942

Although prepared for martyrdom, I preferred that it be postponed.

Winston Churchill

The higher a monkey climbs, the more you see of its behind.

General Joseph "Vinegar Joe" Stilwell

The other day a dog peed on me.

A bad sign.

These are the souls that time men's tries.

Sports Illustrated
… on official timers at track meets

Civilization exists by geological consent, subject to change without notice.

Will Durant

In Biblical times, a man could have as many wives as he could afford. Just like today.

Abigail Van Buren

Always put Horace before Descartes.

Donald O. Rickter

Most of our future lies ahead.

Denny Crum, Louisville basketball coach

We are here on earth to do good to others. What the others are here for, I don't know.

W. H. Auden

There ain't no answer. There ain't going to be any answer. There never has been an answer. That's the answer.

Gertrude Stein

What can you say about a society that says that God is dead and Elvis is alive?

Irv Kupcinet

To Jesus Christ! A splendid chap!

Toast by Sir Ralph Richardson

It's not what you are, it's what you don't become that hurts.

Oscar Levant

The ethical argument regarding abortion hinges on the question of exactly when life begins. Some people believe that life begins at forty.

Kevin Nealon

Everything I did in my life that was worthwhile I caught hell for.

Earl Warren

In a fight between you and the world, bet on the world.

Franz Kafka

In spite of the cost of living, it's still popular.

Kathleen Norris

The optimist proclaims that we live in the best of all possible worlds, and the pessimist fears this is true.

James Branch Cabell

Truth is more of a stranger than fiction.

Mark Twain

It is annoying to be honest to no purpose.

Ovid (43 B.C.–A.D. 18)

I like trees because they seem more resigned to the way they have to live than other things do.

Willa Cather

Many men die at twenty-five and aren't buried until they are seventy-five.

Mae West

Boy meets girl. So what?

Bertolt Brecht

I grew up to have my father's looks, my father's speech patterns, my father's posture, my father's opinions, and my mother's contempt for my father.

Jules Feiffer

It is possible that blondes also prefer gentlemen.

Mamie Van Doren

For birth control I rely on my personality.

Milt Abel

It is a gentleman's first duty to remember in the morning who it was he took to bed with him.

Dorothy L. Sayers

Once while we were making love, a curious optical illusion occurred, and it almost looked as though she were moving.

Woody Allen

I am at two with nature.

Woody Allen

I once made love for an hour and fifteen minutes, but it was the night the clocks are set ahead.

Garry Shandling

Sometimes a cigar is just a cigar.

Sigmund Freud

My mother always phones me and asks, "Is everything all wrong?"

Richard Lewis

I have never understood the fear of some parents about babies getting mixed up in the hospital. What difference does it make as long as you get a good one?

Hey wood Broun

Before I was married I had three theories about raising children. Now I have three children and no theories.

John Wilmot, Earl of Rochester (1647–1680)

Ask your child what he wants for dinner only if he's buying.

Fran Lebowitz

Children despise their parents until the age of forty, when they suddenly become just like them, thus preserving the system.

Quentin Crewe

Santa Claus has the right idea: Visit people once a year.

Victor Borge

Setting a good example for children takes all the fun out of middle age.

William Feather

In order to influence a child, one must be careful not to be that child's parent or grandparent.

Don Marquis

The time not to become a father is eighteen years before a war.

E. B. White

I have over 42,000 children, and not one comes to visit.

Mel Brooks as The 2000-Year-Old Man

Any father whose son raises his hand against him is guilty of having produced a son who raised his hand against him.

Charles Péguy

I've been promoted to middle management. I never thought I'd sink so low.

Tim Gould

No man ever listened himself out of a job.

Calvin Coolidge

Canadians shouldn't come down to Southern California and take jobs away from our Mexicans.

Stanley Ralph Ross

A career is a job that has gone on too long

Jeff MacNelly

A criminal is a person with predatory instincts without sufficient capital to form a corporation.

Howard Scott

Success has many fathers, failure is a mother.

Jeanne Phillips

The worst part of success is trying to find someone who is happy for you.

Bette Midler

If at first you don't succeed, find out if the loser gets anything.

Bill Lyon

To make a small fortune, invest a large fortune.

Bruce Cohn

Formula for success: Rise early, work hard, strike oil.

J. Paul Getty

Money can't buy friends, but it can get you a better class of enemy.

Spike Milligan

The upper crust is a bunch of crumbs held together by dough.

Joseph A. Thomas

I no longer prepare food or drink with more than one ingredient.

Cyra McFadden

The penalty of success is to be bored by the people who used to snub you.

Nancy Astor

I refuse to spend my life worrying about what I eat. There is no pleasure worth forgoing just for an extra three years in the geriatric ward.

John Mortimer

Diets are mainly food for thought.

N. Wylie Jones

The toughest part of being on a diet is shutting up about it.

Gerald Nachman

Meat is murder, but fish is justifiable homicide.

Jeremy Hardy

I'm not a vegetarian because I love animals; I'm a vegetarian because I hate plants.

A. Whitney Brown

Never order anything in a vegetarian restaurant that ordinarily would have meat in it.

Tom Parker

The key to a successful restaurant is dressing girls in degrading clothes.

Michael O'Donoghue

The food in Yugoslavia is either very good or very bad. One day they served us fried chains.

Mel Brooks

The art of medicine, like that of war, is murderous and conjectural.

Voltaire

Winston Churchill 's habit of guzzling a quart or two   a day of good cognac is what saved civilization from the Luftwaffe, Hegelian logic, Wagnerian love-deaths, and potato pancakes.

Charles McCabe

I feel sorry for people who don't drink, because when they get up in the morning, they're not going to feel any better all day.

Frank Sinatra

Politics is a means of preventing people from taking part in what properly concerns them.

Paul Valéry

Democracy is the name we give to the people when we need them.

Robert Pellevé, Marquis de Flers

No more good must be attempted than the public can bear.

Thomas Jefferson

I don't know much about being a millionaire, but I bet I'd be good at it.

Dorothy Parker

Thomas Jefferson's slaves loved him so much they called him by a special name: Dad.

Mark Russell

No matter what your religion, you should try to become a government program, for then you will have everlasting life.

U.S. Representative Lynn Martin

The nice thing about being a celebrity is that, if you bore people, they think it's their fault.

Henry Kissinger

A celebrity is a person known to many people he is glad he doesn't know.

H. L. Mencken

People hate me because I am a multifaceted, talented, wealthy, internationally famous genius.

Jerry Lewis

Every hero becomes a bore at last.

Ralph Waldo Emerson

Baseball is what we were, football is what we have become.

Mary McGrory

No comment.

Doug Moe
... on hearing that he had been voted the most quotable coach in the National Basketball Association

If you are caught on a golf course during a storm and are afraid of lightning, hold up a 1-iron. Not even God can hit a 1-iron.

Lee Trevino

Skiing combines outdoor fun with knocking down trees with your face.

Dave Barry

When I feel athletic, I go to a sports bar.

Paul Clisura

A painter can hang his pictures, but a writer can only hang himself.

Edward Dahlberg

The multitude of books is a great evil. There is no measure or limit to this fever of writing; everyone must be an author, some for some kind of vanity to acquire celebrity and raise a name, others for the sake of lucre or gain.

Martin Luther

A good many young writers make the mistake of enclosing a stamped self-addressed envelope big enough for a manuscript to come back in. This is too much of a temptation for the editor.

Ring Lardner

I love being a writer. It's the paperwork I can't stand.

Peter De Vries

Nice guys can't write.

Literary agent Knox Burger

Either a writer doesn't want to talk about his work, or he talks about it more than you want.

Anatole Broyard

To call Richard Brautigan's poetry doggerel is an insult to the entire canine world.

Lazlo Coakley

I am here to live out loud.

Emile Zola

I sound my barbaric yawp from the rooftops of the world.

Walt Whitman

Nothing stinks like a pile of unpublished writing.

Sylvia Plath

No passion in the world is equal to the passion to alter someone else's draft.

H. G. Wells

Having your book turned into a movie is like seeing your oxen turned into bouillon cubes.

John Le Carré

Writing is a profession in which you have to keep proving your talent to people who have none.

Jules Renard

The New York Times Book Review is alive with the sound of axes grinding.

Gore Vidal

Henry James writes fiction as if it were a painful duty.

Oscar Wilde

I hate books, for they only teach people to talk about what they don't understand.

Jean-Jacques Rousseau

Books should be tried by a judge and jury as though they were crimes.

Samuel Butler

Autobiography is a preemptive strike against biographers.

Barbara Grizzuti Harrison

I'm thirty years old, but I read at the thirty-four- year-old level.
Dana Carvey

Canada is the vichyssoise of nations — it's cold, half French, and difficult to stir.

Stuart Keate

Imagine what it would be like if TV actually were good. It would be the end of everything we know.

Marvin Minsky

America is a mistake, a giant mistake.

Sigmund Freud

Making duplicate copies and computer printouts of things no one wanted even one of in the first place is giving America a new sense of purpose.

Andy Rooney

Americans will put up with anything provided it doesn't block traffic.

Dan Rather

If all the cars in the United States were placed end to end, it would probably be Labor Day Weekend.

Doug Larson

A hick town is one in which there is no place to go where you shouldn't be.

Alexander Woollcott

All creative people should be required to leave California for three months every year.

Gloria Swanson

New York is an exciting town where something is happening all the time, most of it unsolved.

Johnny Carson

An interesting thing about New York City is that the subways run through the sewers.

Garrison Keillor

On a New York subway you get fined for spitting, but you can throw up for nothing.

Lewis Grizzard

New York City is filled with the same kind of people I left New Jersey to get away from.

Fran Lebowitz

If you want to be safe on the streets at night, carry a projector and slides of your last vacation.

Helen Mundis

Art is about making something out of nothing and selling it.

Frank Zappa

I do not seek, I find.

Pablo Picasso

I am a critic — as essential to the theater as ants to a picnic.

Without music, life would be a mistake.

Friedrich Nietzsche

If Beethoven had been killed in a plane crash at the age of twenty-two, it would have changed the history of music. And aviation.

Tom Stoppard

Bach in an hour. Offenbach sooner.

Sign on music store door

I was involved in the Great Folk Music Scare back in the sixties, when it almost caught on.

Martin Mull

We aren't worried about posterity; we want it to sound good right now.

Duke Ellington

If it weren't for the Japanese and Germans, we wouldn't have any good war movies.

Stanley Ralph Ross

War is the unfolding of miscalculations.

Barbara Tuchman

When a thing is funny, search it carefully for a hidden truth.

George Bernard Shaw

You don't stop laughing because you grow old; you grow old because you stop laughing.

Michael Pritchard

O ld age comes at a bad time.

Sue Banducci

If you survive long enough, you're revered — rather like an old building.

Katharine Hepburn

Old age means realizing you will never own all the dogs you wanted to.

Joe Gores

An old man in love is like a flower in winter.

Portuguese proverb

Death is not the end; there remains the litigation.

Ambrose Bierce

No matter how rich you become, how famous or powerful, when you die the size of your funeral will still pretty much depend on the weather.

Michael Pritchard

LAST WILL AND TESTAMENT: I owe much, I have nothing, the rest I leave to the poor.

Rabelais

Next to the originator of a great quote is the first quoter of it. Ralph

Waldo Emerson

I felt sorry for myself because I had no hands until I met a man who had no chips.

Kent G. Andersson

If the rich could hire people to die for them, the poor could make a wonderful living.

Jewish proverb

The prime purpose of eloquence is to keep other people from talking.

Louis Vermeil

There are some things only intellectuals are crazy enough to believe.

George Orwell

ॐ

People performing mime in public should be subject to - citizen's arrest on the theory that the normal First Amendment protection of free speech has in effect been waived by someone who has formally adopted a policy of not speaking.

Calvin Trillin

I've always found paranoia to be a perfectly defensible position.

Pat Conroy

The fuchsia is the world's most carefully spelled flower.

Jimmy Barnes

The days of the digital watch are numbered.

Tom Stoppard

I have never seen a situation so dismal that a policeman couldn't make it worse.

Brendan Behan

If I die, I forgive you; if I live, we'll see.

Spanish proverb

Most conversations are simply monologues delivered in the presence of witnesses.

Margaret Millar

When I can no longer bear to think of the victims of broken homes, I begin to think of the victims of intact ones.

Peter De Vries

To disagree with three-fourths of the British public is one of the first requisites of sanity.

Oscar Wilde

A hat should be taken off when you greet a lady and left off for the rest of your life. Nothing looks more stupid than a hat.

P. J. O'Rourke

Prostitution, like acting, is being ruined by amateurs.

Alexander Woollcott

A good husband is healthy and absent.

Japanese proverb

I'm not a Jew. I'm Jew*ish*. I don't go the whole hog.

Jonathan Miller

Prevailing opinions are generally the opinions of the generation that is passing.

Disraeli

Progress has never been a bargain. You have to pay for it. Sometimes I think there's a man who sits behind a counter and says, "All right, you can have a telephone, but you lose privacy and the charm of distance." "Madam, you may vote but at a price. You lose the right to retreat behind the powder puff or your petticoat." "Mister, you may conquer the air but the birds will lose their wonder and the clouds will smell of gasoline."

Jerome Lawrence and Robert E. Lee, Inherit The Wind

It is dangerous to be right in matters where established men are wrong.

Voltaire

Political correctness does not legislate tolerance; it only organizes hatred.

Jacques Barzun

Let be be the finale of seem.

Wallace Stevens

Opportunities multiply as they are seized.

Sun Tzu

Things which matter most must never be at the mercy of things which matter least.

Goethe

We don't see the world as it is, we see the world as we are.

Anaïs Nin

Every man is guilty of the good he does not do.

Voltaire

You miss 100% of the shots you don't take.

Wayne Gretsky

I love deadlines. I love the whooshing noise they make as they go by.

Douglas Adams

Life is too important to be taken seriously.

Oscar Wilde

Live a good life. If there are gods and they are just, then they will not care how devout you have been, but will welcome you based on the virtues you have lived by. If there are gods, but unjust, then you should not want to worship them. If there are no gods, then you will be gone, but will have lived a noble life that will live on in the memories of your loved ones.

Marcus Aurelius, Meditations

It is not the critic who counts; not the man who points out how the strong man stumbles, or where the doer of deeds could have done them better. The credit belongs to the man who is actually in the arena, whose face is marred by dust and sweat and blood; who strives valiantly; who errs, who comes short again and again, because there is no effort without error and shortcoming; but who does actually strive to do the deeds; who knows great enthusiasms, the great devotions; who spends himself in a worthy cause; who at the best knows in the end the triumph of high achievement, and who at the worst, if he fails, at least fails while daring greatly, so that his place shall never be with those cold and timid souls who neither know victory nor defeat.

Theodore Roosevelt

The deeper that sorrow carves into your being, the more joy you can contain..

Kahlil Gibran

Censorship is telling a man he can't eat a steak because a baby can't chew it.

Mark Twain

Be who you are and say what you feel, because those who mind don't matter, and those who matter don't mind.

Dr. Seuss

It is the mark of an educated mind to be able to entertain a thought without accepting it.

Aristotle

A witty saying proves nothing.

Voltaire

The greatest argument against democracy is a five minute conversation with the average voter.

Winston Churchill

In the end, we remember not the words of our enemies, but the silence of our friends.

Martin Luther King Jr

The mark of the immature man is that he wants to die nobly for a cause, while the mark of a mature man is that he wants to live humbly for one.

Wilhelm Stekel

Though lovers be lost, love shall not. And death shall have no dominion.

Dylan Thomas

In the depth of winter, I finally learned that within me there lay an invincible summer.

Albert Camus.

Assistant: Mr. Stevenson all of the smart people are going to vote for you!

Adlai Stevenson: Yes but I need a majority

First they ignore you, then they laugh at you, then they fight you, then you win.

Ghandi

I would never die for my beliefs because I might be wrong.

Bertrand Russell

If, after I depart this vale, you ever remember me and have thought to please my ghost, forgive some sinner and wink your eye at some homely girl.

H.L. Mencken

I don't take drugs, I ***am*** drugs.

Salvador Dali

Those who were seen dancing were thought to be insane by those who could not hear the music.

Nietzsche

The one thing you can't take away from me is the way I choose to respond to what you do to me. The last of one's freedoms is to choose one's attitude in any given circumstance.

Viktor Frankl

All men dream, but not equally. Those who dream by night in the dusty recesses of their minds, wake in the day to find that it was vanity: but the dreamers of the day are dangerous men, for they may act on their dreams with open eyes, to make them possible.

T.E. Lawrence

I don't judge a man's success by how high he climbs, but by how high he bounces when he hits the bottom.

Gen. George S. Patton

If I find in myself desires which nothing in this world can satisfy, the only logical explanation is that I was made for another world.

C.S. Lewis

She said the word happy as if she were looking at it from a great distance through a telescope.

Richard Brautigan

A dwarf is not tall though he stands on a mountaintop; a giant keeps his height though he stands in a well.

Seneca

Bigger is not better; slower may be faster; less may well prove more.

Ernest T. Campbell

If you think there's a solution, you're part of the problem.

George Carlin

Quite often in history action has been the echo of words. An era of talk was followed by an era of events.

Eric Hoffer

Sir, I am not a descendant. I am an ancestor.

John Churchill, 1ˢᵗ Duke of Marlborough

Trend is Not Destiny.

Lewis Mumford

The hottest places in Hell are reserved for those who, in a time of great moral crisis, maintain their neutrality.

Dante

The worst moment for an atheist is when he is truly thankful and has nobody to thank.

D.G. Rosetti

A great artist is always before his time, or behind it.

George Moore

What is a cult? It's just not enough people to make a minority.

Robert Altman

When you are on a sinking ship, your thoughts will be about sinking ships.

George Orwell

All truth is old, and only poets, liars, and fools can be original.

Will Durant

Love thy enemies, in case thy friends turn out to be a bunch of bastards.

R.A. Dickson

A professor must have a theory, as a dog must have fleas.

H.L. Mencken

Let those that play your clowns speak no more than is set down for them.

Hamlet

Money is the sixth sense that enables us to enjoy the other five.

Somerset Maugham

He who has never hoped can never despair.

George Bernard Shaw, Caesar and Cleopatra.

The young always have the same problem – how to rebel and conform at the same time. They have solved this by defying their parents and copying one another.

Quentin Crisp

In the Third Reich, one Nazi procession included a small, sad contingent of Jews carrying a banner inscribed, "Down With Us."

Malcolm Muggridge

Our bloods,

Of cobur, weight, and heat, pour'd all together,

Would quite confound distinction...

Honours thrive

When rather from our acts we them derive

Than our foregoers.

William Shakespeare, All's Well That Ends Well

Conventions are customs which are more practiced than preached. Morals are customs which are more preached than practiced.

Will Durant, Pleasures of Philosophy.

Man is born in chains, and is everywhere free.

Malcolm Muggeridge

I don't know, I don't care, and it doesn't matter anyway.

Jack Kerouac

A comedian knows just what he is saying, but he doesn't mean it. A poet might not know what he is saying, but he means every word.

Whitman McGowan

Hell is other people.

Jean Paul Sartre

A little knowledge separates us from God, much knowledge brings us back. We must not be afraid to go too far, for the truth is beyond.

Proust

Whenever you see 'No Exit', it means there is an exit.

Hugh Kingsmill

You cannot sleep with all the women in the world but you *must* try.

Pushkin

Science is what you know. Philosophy is what you don't know.

Bertrand Russell

A married man will do anything for money.

Talleyrand

Satire is the sour milk of human kindness.

George Agassiz

Wives may come and go, but ex-wives are forever.

Joe Bob Briggs

I feel like a fugitive from the law of averages.

Bill Madden

Ennui, felt on the proper occasions, is a sign of intelligence.

Clifton Fauman

A little madness in the spring,

Is wholesome even for the king.

Emily Dickinson

Reasonable people adapt themselves to the world. Unreasonable people attempt to adapt the world to themselves. All Progress, therefore, depends on unreasonable people.

George Bernard Shaw

If I can't be a good example, I might as well be a horrible warning.

Catherine Aird

There is either a forgery or a damn clever original!

Frank Sullivan

The greatest masterpiece in literature is only a dictionary out of order. –

Jean Cocteau

It's paradise, if you can stand it.

Gertrude Stein, on Mallorca

On the continent the works of Shakespeare are honored in a double way: by the admiration of Italy and Germany, and by the contempt of the French.

Coleridge

The trouble with Oakland is there's no there there.

Gertrude Stein

The trouble with Oakland is that, when you get there, it's there.

Herb Caen

Who says this thing is new? For the dreams of man are older than brooding Tyre, or the contemplative Sphinx, or garden-girdled Babylon; and I fashioned this thing in my dreams.

H.P. Lovecraft

L ook how much faster and cheaper the machines can reproduce the new inferior product! Naturally it was difficult for them to even consider that it might be better to produce something of worth in an inefficient way than to produce worthless things efficiently. Efficiency was everything. Beauty became Utility; Joy became Laughter; Creation became Labor; Art became Productive; and Man became Machine. It is this disaster that some would define as Progress. James Drought,

Drugoth, 1965

In Italy, for thirty years under the Borgias, they had warfare, terror, murder and bloodshed, but they produced Michelangelo, Leonardo da Vinci and the Renaissance. In Switzerland, they had brotherly love, they had five hundred years of democracy and peace – and what did that produce? The cuckoo clock.

Orson Welles

My doctor told me to stop having intimate dinners for four. Unless there are three other people.

Orson Welles

I passionately hate the idea of being with it, I think an artist has always to be out of step with his time.

Orson Welles

If you want a happy ending, it just depends on where you close the book.

Orson Welles

Style is knowing who you are, what you want to say, and not giving a damn.

Orson Welles

I don't pray really, because I don't want to bore God.

Orson Welles

I do not believe the people who tell me they do not care a row of pins for the opinion of their fellows. It is the bravado of ignorance. They meanonly that they do not fear reproaches for peccadillos which they are convinced none will discover.

W. Somerset Maugham

It's a very funny thing about life; if you refuse to accept anything but the best, you very often get it.

W. Somerset Maugham

One can be very much in love with a woman without wishing to spend the rest of one's life with her.

W. Somerset Maugham

The love that lasts the longest is the love that is never returned.

W. Somerset Maugham

Death is a very dull, dreary affair, and my advice to you is to have nothing whatsoever to do with it.

W. Somerset Maugham

The secret to life is meaningless unless you discover it yourself.

W. Somerset Maugham

Women are constantly trying to commit suicide for love, but generally they take care not to succeed.

W. Somerset Maugham

Love is what happens to men and women who don't know each other.

W. Somerset Maugham

If nobody spoke unless he had something to say, the human race would very soon lose the use of speech.

W. Somerset Maugham

It wasn't until late in life that I discovered how easy it is to say "I don't know".

W. Somerset Maugham

My own belief is that there is hardly anyone whose sexual life, if it were broadcast, would not fill the world at large with surprise and horror.

W. Somerset Maugham

It is one of the defects of my character that I cannot altogether dislike anyone who makes me laugh.

W. Somerset Maugham

When people are no good at anything else they become writers.

W. Somerset Maugham

The unfortunate thing about this world is that good habits are so much easier to give up than bad ones.

W. Somerset Maugham

What do we any of us have but our illusions? And what do we ask of others but that we be allowed to keep them?

W. Somerset Maugham

Money is like a sixth sense without which you cannot make a complete use of the other five.

W. Somerset Maugham

A woman can forgive a man for the harm he does her...but she can never forgive him for the sacrifices he makes on her account.

W. Somerset Maugham

We are foolish and sentimental and melodramatic at twenty-five, but if we weren't perhaps we should be less wise at fifty.

W. Somerset Maugham

Art is merely the refuge which the ingenious have invented, when they were supplied with food and women, to escape the tediousness of life.

W. Somerset Maugham

You are not angry with people when you laugh at them. Humor teaches tolerance.

W. Somerset Maugham

The Tasmanians, who never committed adultery, are now extinct.

W. Somerset Maugham

There is a certain elegance in wasting time. Any fool can waste money, but when you waste time you waste what is priceless.

W. Somerset Maugham

Our envy always lasts longer than the happiness of those we envy.

La Rochefoucauld

We only confess our little faults to persuade people that we have no big ones.

La Rochefoucauld

We should not be upset that others hide the truth from us, when we hide it so often from ourselves.

La Rochefoucauld

If we had no faults, we should not take so much pleasure in noting those of others.

La Rochefoucauld

Old men delight in giving good advice as a consolation for the fact that they can no longer provide bad examples.

La Rochefoucauld

We would rather speak ill of ourselves than not talk about ourselves at all.

La Rochefoucauld

The refusal of praise is only the wish to be praised twice.

La Rochefoucauld

Hypocrisy is an homage that vice pays to virtue.

La Rochefoucauld

It is less dangerous to treat most men badly than to treat them too well.

La Rochefoucauld

We often forgive those who bore us, but we cannot forgive those whom we bore.

La Rochefoucauld

It is easier to know man than to know one man.

La Rochefoucauld

All these health nuts will feel silly one day, laying in the hospital dying of nothing.

Redd Foxx

Politics, amidst the interests of the imagination, are a pistol shot in the middle of a concert. This noise is ear-rending, without being forceful. It clashes with every instrument.

Stendhal

Battle not with monsters, lest ye become a monster, and if you stare into the abyss, the abyss stares back.

Nietzsche

W hat the world needs is more geniuses with humility, there are so few of us left.

Oscar Levant

Happiness isn't something you experience, it's something you remember.

Oscar Levant

It's not what you are, it's what you don't become that hurts.

Oscar Levant

Underneath this flabby exterior is an enormous lack of character.

Oscar Levant

There is a thin line between genius and insanity. I have erased this line.

Oscar Levant

I have a sixth sense; I lack the other five.

Oscar Levant

I envy people who drink — at least they know what to blame everything on.

Oscar Levant

Failure has gone to his head.

Wilson Mizner

Steal from one author, it's plagiarism; steal from many, it's research.

Wilson Mizner

God help those who do not help themselves.

Wilson Mizner

The cuckoo who is on to himself is halfway out of the clock.

Wilson Mizner

I respect faith, but doubt is what gets you an education.

Wilson Mizner

A good listener is not only popular everywhere, but after a while he knows something.

Wilson Mizner

Be nice to people on your way up because you'll meet the same people on your way down.

Wilson Mizner

Those who welcome death have only tried it from the ears up.

Wilson Mizner

Working in Hollywood is a trip through a sewer in a glassbottom boat.

Wilson Mizner

Treat a whore like a lady — and a lady like a whore.

Wilson Mizner

I've always regarded it as a test of character to dislike the Kennedys. I don't really respect anyone who falls for Camelot.

Christopher Hitchens

I t is not enough to succeed. Others must fail.

Gore Vidal

Every time a friend succeeds, I die a little.

Gore Vidal

A writer must always tell the truth, unless he's a journalist.

Gore Vidal

Never pass up a chance to have sex or appear on television.

Gore Vidal

Andy Warhol is the only genius I've ever known with an IQ of 60.

Gore Vidal

I 've been using cocaine for twenty years, and it's never become a habit with me.

Tallulah Bankhead

I've tried several varieties of sex. The conventional position makes me claustrophobic and the others give me a stiff neck or lockjaw.

Tallulah Bankhead

If I had to live my life again, I'd make the same mistakes, only sooner.

Tallulah Bankhead

(On seeing a former lover for the first time in years) I thought I told you to wait in the car.

Tallulah Bankhead

Only good girls keep diaries. Bad girls don't have time.

Tallulah Bankhead

I'll come and make love to you at five o'clock. If I'm late start without me.

Tallulah Bankhead

Here's a rule I recommend. Never practice two vices at once.

Tallulah Bankhead

T he free-lance writer is a man who is paid per piece or per word or perhaps.

Robert Benchley

A dog teaches a boy fidelity, perseverance, and to turn around three times before lying down.

Robert Benchley

Anyone can do any amount of work, provided it isn't the work he is supposed to be doing.

Robert Benchley

Opera is when a guy gets stabbed in the back and, instead of bleeding, he sings.

Robert Benchley

There are two kinds of people in the world, those who believe there are two kinds of people in the world and those who don't.

Robert Benchley

Avoid crowds. This applies to all times of the year. You never know who may be in a crowd, and mingling with one may result in your being reminded of an old fifty-dollar loan or a promise to drop in and hear someone sing.

Robert Benchley

Does the average man get enough sleep? What is enough sleep? What is the average man? What is does?

Robert Benchley

They sicken of the calm, who know the storm.

Dorothy Parker

The two most beautiful words in the English language are "check enclosed."

Dorothy Parker

Wit has truth in it; wise-cracking is simply calisthenics with words.

Dorothy Parker

You can't teach an old dogma new tricks.

Dorothy Parker

Sorrow is tranquility remembered in emotion.

Dorothy Parker

The cure for boredom is curiosity. There is no cure for curiosity.

Dorothy Parker

If you want to know what God thinks of money, just look at the people he gave it to.

Dorothy Parker

I require only three things of a man. He must be handsome, ruthless and stupid.

Dorothy Parker

I don't care what is written about me so long as it isn't true.

Dorothy Parker

I'm never going to be famous. My name will never be writ large on the roster of Those Who Do Things. I don't do any thing. Not one single thing. I used to bite my nails, but I don't even do that any more.

Dorothy Parker

The only ism Hollywood believes in is plagiarism.

Dorothy Parker

The tragedy of life is not that man loses, but that he almost wins.

Heywood Broun

A bsurdity, n. A statement or belief manifestly inconsistent with one's own opinion.

Ambrose Bierce

Abstainer, n. A weak person who yields to the temptation of denying himself a pleasure. A total abstainer is one who abstains from everything but abstention, and especially from inactivity in the affairs of others.

Ambrose Bierce

Acquaintance, n. A person whom we know well enough to borrow from, but not well enough to lend to. A degree of friendship called slight when its object is poor or obscure, and intimate when he is rich or famous.

Ambrose Bierce

Admiration, n. Our polite recognition of another's resemblance to ourselves.

Ambrose Bierce

Christian, n. One who believes that the New Testament is a divinely inspired book admirably suited to the spiritual needs of his neighbor. One who follows the teachings of Christ so long as they are not inconsistent with a life of sin.

Ambrose Bierce

Congratulation, n. The civility of envy.

Ambrose Bierce

Conservative, n. A statesman enamored of existing evils, as opposed to a Liberal, who wants to replace them with others.

Ambrose Bierce

Happiness, n. An agreeable sensation arising from contemplating the misery of another.

Ambrose Bierce

Once, adj. Enough.

Ambrose Bierce

Positive, adj. Mistaken at the top of one's voice.

Ambrose Bierce

Pray, v. To ask that the laws of the universe be annulled in behalf of a single petitioner confessedly unworthy.

Ambrose Bierce

If you would be accounted great by your contemporaries, be not too much greater than they.

Ambrose Bierce

Defenceless, adj. Unable to attack.

Ambrose Bierce

Corporation, n. An ingenious device for obtaining individual profit without individual responsibility.

Ambrose Bierce

You are not permitted to kill a woman who has wronged you, but nothing forbids you to reflect that she is growing older every minute. You are avenged 1440 times a day.

Ambrose Bierce

I'd like to leave you on a positive note -- but would you settle for two negatives?

Woody Allen

It ain't me man, it's the system.

Charles Manson

Walt Disney has the best casting. If he doesn't like an actor he just tears him up.

Alfred Hitchcock

The whole sordid business began on a bleak November afternoon a couple of years ago in Philadelphia, a metropolis sometimes known as the City of Brotherly Love but more accurately as the City of Bleak November Afternoons.

S.J. Perelman, Westward Ha!

A nation that makes a great distinction between its scholars and its warriors will have its laws made by cowards and its wars fought by fools.

Thucydides

Americans mumble correct pronunciations while the British clearly articulate faulty ones.

Peter De Vries

Everybody hates me because I'm so universally liked.

Peter de Vries

Life is a zoo in a jungle.

Peter De Vries

The rich aren't like us, they pay less taxes.

Peter De Vries

We must love one another, yes, yes, that's all true enough, but nothing says we have to like each other.

Peter De Vries

The satirist shoots to kill while the humorist brings his prey back alive and eventually releases him again for another chance.

Peter De Vries

Gluttony is an emotional escape, a sign something is eating us.

Peter De Vries

The bonds of matrimony are like any other bonds - they mature slowly.

Peter De Vries

My father hated radio and could not wait for television to be invented so he could hate that too.

Peter De Vries

Nostalgia isn't what it used to be.

Peter De Vries

The murals in restaurants are on par with the food in museums.

Peter De Vries

There are times when parenthood seems nothing but feeding the mouth that bites you.

Peter De Vries

The universe is like a safe to which there is a combination. But the combination is locked up in the safe.

Peter De Vries

I wanted to be bored to death, as good a way to go as any.

Peter De Vrie

Well man, I may be in the middle of all this shit, but I certainly don't want any part of it.

Jack Kerouac

The only thing more boring than track, is field.

Dan Jenkins

We don't stop playing because we grow old; we grow old because we stop playing.

George Bernard Shaw

Age is an issue of mind over matter. If you don't mind, it doesn't matter.

Mark Twain

The old believe everything: the middle-aged suspect everything: the young know everything.

Oscar Wilde

By working faithfully eight hours a day you may eventually get to be boss and work twelve hours a day.

Robert Frost

Only the wisest and stupidest of men never change.

Confucius

Always be nice to your children because they are the ones who will choose your rest home.

Phyllis Diller

It takes courage to grow up and turn out to be who you really are.

e e cummings

To repeat what others have said requires education. To challenge it requires brains.

Marry Pettibone Poole

A bank is a place where they lend you an umbrella in fair weather and ask for it back when it begins to rain.

Robert Frost

Opera is when a guy gets stabbed in the back and, instead of bleeding, he sings.

Ed Gardner

War is a cowardly escape from the problems of peace.

Thomas Mann

Failure is simply the opportunity to begin again, this time more intelligently.

Henry Ford

Success is walking from failure to failure with no loss of enthusiasm.

Winston Churchill

I don't know the key to success, but the key to failure is trying to please everybody.

Bill Cosby

You can do anything, but not everything.

David Allen

"Whom are you?" he asked, for he had attended business college.

George Ade

We are talking now of summer evenings in Knoxville, Tennessee, in the time that I lived there so successfully disguised to myself as a child.

James Agee

We know that the nature of genius is to provide idiots with ideas twenty years later.

Louis Aragon

An expert is a person who has made all the mistakes that can be made in a very narrow field.

Niels Bohr

The urge to save humanity is almost always a false front for the urge to rule.

H.L. Mencken

Talking about music is like dancing about architechture.

Frank Zappa

The first lesson of economics is scarcity: there is never enough of anything to fully satisfy all those who want it. The first lesson of politics is to disregard the first lesson of economics.

Thomas Sowell

If you have always believed that everyone should play by the same rules and be judged by the same standards, that would have gotten you labeled a radical 60 years ago, a liberal 30 years ago and a racist today.

Thomas Sowell

Worse is the new normal.

Mark Steyn

The streets were dark with something more than night.

Raymond Chandler

Ain't no man can avoid being born average, but there ain't no man got to be common.

Satchel Paige

Life can only be understood backwards; but it must be lived forwards.

Soren Kierkegaard

You can learn many things from children. How much patience you have, for instance.

Franklin P. Adams

The hardest thing to learn in life is which bridge to cross and which to burn.

David Russell

The most difficult thing in the world is to know how to do a thing and to watch someone else do it wrong, without comment.

T. H. White

Men occassionally stumble over the truth, but most of them pick themselves up and hurry on as if nothing had happened.

Winston Churchill

Nearly all men can stand adversity, but if you want to test a man's character, give him power.

Abraham Lincoln

On the whole, human beings want to be good, but not too good and not quite all the time.

George Orwell

If you can spend a perfectly useless afternoon in a perfectly useless manner, you have learned how to live.

Lin Yutang

A dead thing can go with the stream, but only a living thing can go against it.

G. K. Chesterton

When you are younger you get blamed for crimes you never committed and when you're older you begin to get credit for virtues you never possessed. It evens itself out.

George Santayana

Life is like playing a violin in public and learning the instrument as one goes on.

Samuel Butler

All life is 6 to 5 against.

Damon Runyon

Life consists not in holding good cards but in playing those you hold well.

Josh Billings

Do well and you will have no need for ancestors.

Voltaire

People travel to wonder at the height of the mountains, at the huge waves of the seas, at the long course of the rivers, at the vast compass of the ocean, at the circular motion of the stars, and yet they pass by themselves without wondering.

Saint Augustine

We are here to laugh at the odds and live our lives so well that Death will tremble to take us.

Charles Bukowski

Death is nothing to us, since when we are, death has not come, and when death has come, we are not.

Epicurus

Live so that you wouldn't be ashamed to sell the family parrot to the town gossip.

Will Rogers

You are never too old to be what you might have been.

George Eliot

The trouble with quotes about death is that 99.999 percent of them are made by people who are still alive.

Joshua Bruns

I have discovered that all human evil comes from this: man's being unable to sit still and quiet in a room alone.

Blaise Pascal

The years between fifty and seventy are the hardest. You are always being asked to do things, and yet you are not decrepit enough to turn them down.

T. S. Eliot

The only man who behaves sensibly is my tailor; he takes my measure anew every time he sees me, whilst all the rest go on with their old measurements, and expect them to fit me.

George Bernard Shaw

Millions long for immortality who do not know what to do with themselves on a rainy Sunday afternoon.

Susan Ertz

The tragedy of life is not so much what men suffer, but rather what they miss.

Thomas Carlyle

The greatest thing in life is to die young-but delay it as long as possible.

George Bernard Sbaw

Judge a man by his questions rather than his answers.

Voltaire

Good advice is something a man gives when he is too old to set a bad example.

Francois de La Rochefoucauld

How wonderful it is that nobody need wait a single moment before starting to improve the world.

Anne Frank

What the superior man seeks is in himself. What the mean man seeks is in others.

Confucius

Everything should be as simple as possible, but not simpler.

Albert Einstein

To do just the opposite is also a form of imitation.

Georg Christoph Lichtenberg

We can easily forgive a child who is afraid of the dark. The real tragedy of life is when men are afraid of the light.

Plato

We don't see things as they are, we see them as we are.

Anais Nin

Three o'clock is always too late or too early for anything you want to do.

Jean-Paul Sartre

To err is human; to forgive, infrequent.

Franklin P. Adams

Friendship is born at that moment when one person says to another: What! You, too? I thought I was the only one.

C. S. Lewis

The secret of successful managing is to keep the five guys who hate you away from the four guys who haven't made up their minds.

Casey Stengel

It is necessary for us to learn from others' mistakes. You will not live long enough to make them all yourself.

Admiral Hyman Rickover

Millions saw the apple fall, but Newton was the one who asked why.

Bernard Baruch

Any fool can make things bigger, more complex, and more violent. It takes a touch of genius-and a lot of courage-to move in the opposite direction.

Albert Einstein

You can get a lot farther with a kind word and a gun than a kind word alone.

Al Capone

"Where shall I begin, please, your Majesty?" he asked. "Begin at the beginning," the King said, gravely, "and go on till you come to the end: then stop."

Lewis Carroll

For myself I am an optimist -- it does not seem to be much use being anything else.

Winston Churchill

Annual income twenty pounds, annual expenditure nineteen pounds and six, result happiness. Annual income twenty pounds, annual expenditure twenty pounds ought and six, result misery.

Charles Dickens

Always do sober what you said you'd do drunk. That will teach you to keep your mouth shut

Ernest Hemingway

Anywhere is walking distance, if you've got the time.

Steven Wright

When you reach the top, keep climbing.

Zen aphorism

It is impossible to defeat an ignorant man in argument.

William G. McAdoo

The test of a first-rate intelligence is the ability to hold two opposed ideas in the mind at the same time, and still retain the ability to function. One should, for example, be able to see that things are hopeless and yet be determined to make them otherwise.

F. Scott Fitzgerald

An intellectual is a man who says a simple thing in a difficult way; an artist is a man who says a difficult thing in a simple way.

Charles Bukowski

Poor is the pupil who does not surpass his master.

Leonardo da Vinci

What really knocks me out is a book that, when you're all done reading it, you wish the author that wrote it was a terrific friend of yours and you could call him up on the phone whenever you felt like it. That doesn't happen much, though.

J. D. Salinger

He who asks is a fool for five minutes, but he who does not ask remains a fool forever.

Chinese proverb

I never know whether to congratulate or pity a man on coming to his senses.

William Makepeace Thackeray

When a man you like switches from what he said a year ago, or four years ago, he is a broad-minded person who has courage enough to change his mind with changing conditions. When a man you don't like does it, he is a liar who has broken his promises.

Franklin P. Adams

If liberty means anything at all, it means the right to tell people what they do not want to hear.

George Orwell

If we do not believe in freedom of speech for those we despise we do not believe in it at all.

Noam Chomsky

A country can be judged by the quality of its proverbs.

German proverb

A quiet fool is half a sage.

Yiddish proverb

Since the house is on fire, let us warm ourselves.

Italian proverb

Dance as if no one's watching, sing as if no one's listening, and live everyday as if it were your last.

Irish proverb

At the end of the game, the king and the pawn go back in the same box.

Italian proverb

The church is close, but the road is icey. The tavern is far, but I will walk carefully.

Russian proverb

A man is not honest simply because he never had a chance to steal.

Russian proverb

He who is outside his door has the hardest part of his journey behind him.

Flemish proverb

One meets his destiny in the road he takes to avoid it.

French proverb

If you want people to think you are wise, agree with them.

Yiddish proverb

I'm not against the police, I'm just afraid of them.

Alfred Hitchcock

Blondes make the best victims – they're like virgin snow that shows up the bloody footprints.

Alfred Hitchcock

The length of the film should be directly related to the endurance of the human bladder.

Alfred Hitchcock

I enjoy playing the audience like a piano.

Alfred Hitchcock

Drama is life with the dull bits cut out.

Alfred Hitchcock

www.ingramcontent.com/pod-product-compliance
Lightning Source LLC
Chambersburg PA
CBHW050127280326
41933CB00010B/1285